JB JOSSEY-BASS

THE MOST **EXTREME** ANIMALS

Animal Planet

By Sherry Gerstein

Foreword by Kevin Mohs and Ian McGee

BICENTENNIAL
1807
WILEY
2007
BICENTENNIAL

John Wiley & Sons, Inc.

Published by Jossey-Bass
A Wiley Imprint
989 Market Street, San Francisco, CA 94103-1741
www.josseybass.com

Developed by Nancy Hall, Inc.
Photo research by Linda Falken
Designed by Alisa Komsky and Tom Koken
Cover design by Alisa Komsky

DCI Book Development Team:
Maureen Smith, Executive Vice President & General Manager, Animal Planet
Kevin Mohs, Vice President, Animal Genre, Discovery US Networks Production
Peggy Ang, Vice President, Animal Planet Marketing
Ian McGee, Series Producer, Natural History New Zealand
Carol LeBlanc, Vice President, Licensing
Elizabeth Bakacs, Vice President, Creative Services
Caitlin Erb, Licensing Specialist

Jossey-Bass books and products are available through most bookstores. To contact Jossey-Bass directly, call our Customer Care Department within the U.S. at 800-956-7739, outside the U.S. at 317-572-3986, or fax 317-572-4002.

Jossey-Bass also publishes its books in a variety of electronic formats. Some content that appears in print may not be available in electronic books.

Library of Congress Cataloging-in-Publication Data

Gerstein, Sherry.
 Animal Planet : the most extreme animals / by Sherry Gerstein ; foreword by Kevin Mohs and Ian McGee. — 1st ed.
    p. cm.
 Includes index.
 ISBN: 978-0-7879-8662-9 (cloth)
1. Animals—Juvenile literature. 2. Animals—Adaptation—Juvenile literature. I. Animal Planet (Television network) II. Title.
 QL49.G47 2007
 591.5—dc22
                            2006035891

Printed in China
First edition

10 9 8 7 6 5 4 3 2 1

REACH OUT. ACT. RESPOND.
Go to AnimalPlanet.com/ROAR and find out how you can be a voice for animals everywhere!

TABLE of CONTENTS

Foreword

To me, countdown shows are addictive, because I feel compelled to watch until the very end to discover who or what ranks number one in a given category—even if it's dance moves that changed the world. Given that and my knowledge of animals, it's not surprising that I decided to propose a countdown series about the most amazing behaviors and abilities of all kinds of creatures to Animal Planet. The network liked the idea, so I teamed up with Ian McGee, an entomologist turned television producer for Natural History New Zealand, who once measured caterpillar heads for a living—and *The Most Extreme* was born.

To make the series fun and interactive as well as informative, Ian and I made sure that each show had a unique ranking system that allowed us to include some of the world's wackiest animal behavior. That's how a snail ended up in our "Speed" episode (the cone shell snail moves at lightning speed when it fires its deadly harpoon).

Animal Planet The Most Extreme books follow the same format as the show and are filled with offbeat facts about animals and the astonishing things they do—such as decorator crabs who clip bits of plants or sponges to their shells for camouflage and change their "outfit" whenever they move to blend in with their new surroundings; and chameleons, who change color not to match their surroundings, as many people think, but to match their mood.

Ian, the production team, and I all share a passion for animals, so *The Most Extreme* series has been a filmmaker's dream come true, and we are delighted that there are now books based on the series. If, after watching the show or reading the books, you find yourself sharing unusual animal facts or debating the selections in a *Most Extreme* countdown with friends or family, then Ian and I feel that we have succeeded, because we've not only entertained you, but also engaged you in the extraordinary natural world that surrounds you. So get ready to take reading to the *Most Extreme* as you delve into the pages of *Animal Planet The Most Extreme Animals*, a totally awesome book.

Sincerely,

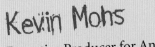

Kevin Mohs

Executive Producer for Animal Planet

Ian McGee

Series Producer for
Natural History New Zealand

You Can't Make This Stuff Up!

WE don't make these headlines up. We don't have to. Earth and its creatures are amazing enough all on their very own. That's because Earth really is a planet of extremes. Extreme weather. Extreme places. Extreme animals.

SPECIAL REPORT:
Toad mother gives birth to hundreds— from her back!

Earth teems with animals of every conceivable size, shape, and color— animals that have reshaped themselves to make the most of their often extreme surroundings in some pretty ingenious ways. From their extreme births to living deaths, we're sharing these extremely incredible stories.

Read on and prepare to be amazed. Extremely amazed.

SPECIAL REPORT:
Hippopotamus attacks and sinks boat!

1 Baby, It's You

aking babies: It's a top priority of every creature on Earth. We already know that having human babies can involve some pretty hard labor. Animal parents have war stories of their own to relate when it comes to birthing babies. So breathe deep, count to ten—and prepare to read ten of the most extreme baby stories in the animal world.

#10

Cuckoo

Life is sweet for a parasitic cuckoo mom. She stakes out the nest of a host bird, lays her egg, and leaves. The host bird incubates the cuckoo egg along with her own, but the cuckoo chick hatches first and pushes the other eggs out of the nest. That means more food for the cuckoo—who will grow to be ten times the size of its foster parents. What happens when the host removes a cuckoo egg from its nest? The mother cuckoo apparently keeps tabs on its eggs and destroys the nests of hosts that don't cooperate!

Many cuckoos have evolved to match the pattern and color of their eggs to that of their host bird.

THAT'S WILD!

#9

Kiwi

This flightless bird from New Zealand has it tough in the baby department. After the female produces a whopper of an egg—up to one-fourth of her own body weight—she goes off for a well-deserved break, and dad takes over, keeping the egg safe and warm for nearly three months—and losing nearly 20 percent of his body weight in the process. Once the kiwi chick is hatched, it can look after itself within just a few days.

#8

Right Whale

A female right whale swims 4,000 miles to find waters warm enough to have her baby. And what a baby it is! A right whale calf weighs in at just over a ton—however, it's born without heat-retaining blubber. Mom has to help the baby build up blubber by stuffing it with extremely rich, high-fat milk. She produces so much milk that one day's supply equals the amount of milk a human baby will consume in a whole year.

#7

Nine-banded Armadillo

Wouldn't it be great to plan to have your baby at exactly the right time? That's what the nine-banded armadillo can do. If food is scarce, the female can delay implantation of her fertilized egg for up to three years. Once implantation occurs, the egg splits into four separate individuals, resulting in the birth of identical quadruplets of the same sex.

#6

Rabbit

A female rabbit, or doe, is ready to have babies at six months of age, and when that happens, she can make a brand-new family of six babies every month for the next ten years. That works out to nearly 700 babies over her lifetime. How does a rabbit mom manage? She doesn't put much energy into tending her babies once they are born, visiting and nursing them for only about ten minutes per day.

#5

Naked Mole Rat

Although they are mammals, these 3-inch-long rodents live in colonies that are similar to those of termites. Only one female—the queen—breeds for the colony, and she's a true specialist. She can have 27 pups in a single litter! But since she has to stay slim and trim in order to squeeze through narrow underground tunnels, she makes her body longer instead of fatter. Hormones trigger an extra growth spurt, lengthening the distance between the bones in her back by an extra 30 percent. The queen also uses hormones to suppress the fertility of the colony's other females.

A naked mole rat's jaws are so powerful they can chew through steel!

THAT'S WILD!

#4

Aphid

"Who needs men?" is an idea that the aphid, a tiny plant-feeding insect, has taken to extremes. For most of a female aphid's life, she reproduces asexually, without help from a partner. She gives birth to one live young and that offspring is usually a female—who is born already pregnant with the next generation! As the season progresses and the weather turns cooler, breeding females start having male babies. When this happens, the males and females mate to produce eggs, which can last through the cold of winter.

Ants often "farm" aphids for their honeydew, a sweet liquid they secrete. In return for the honeydew, the ants protect the aphids from predators such as ladybugs.

THAT'S WILD!

Surinam Toad

Surinam toad moms raise an entire brood of about 100 babies—from egg to fully formed toadlet—on their backs, quite literally! It starts with a mating dance. When the female is ready, the male grabs her around the waist. Together, the pair swims in a circle. At the top of the circle, the female releases her eggs and the male releases his sperm. The couple swims back to the bottom of the circle, and the female is now ready to catch the fertilized eggs on her back, while the male taps them into place. They repeat the process a few times for a total of about 100 eggs. Special hormones kick in to make the skin on the female's back swell up and harden around the eggs to protect them while the babies develop. When the babies are ready to emerge, the mother helps by molting, or shedding her skin. She can even exert pressure to help them out.

Get off my back!

Surinam toads have no tongues! They use their sensitive fingertips to forage for food on the bottoms of ponds and rivers.

THAT'S WILD!

He has his father's nose!

#2 Seahorse

If your father gives birth to you, does that make him your mother? For the answer to this confusing question, look no further than the seahorse. This tiny fish has a fairly normal courtship. It's how the eggs are fertilized that makes the seahorse's approach to giving birth so unique. The female makes so many eggs that she has little energy left to watch over them, so she turns the job over to her mate. Using a long egg tube, she deposits her eggs in a brood pouch on the male's belly. He then fertilizes them and keeps them safe until they are ready to hatch. The male even regulates the amount of salt in the brood pouch, slowly increasing it to match the outside water, so the babies won't experience too much shock when they emerge. The developing eggs get some nutrients from the lining of the brood pouch. When the babies are ready to be born, the male even has contractions to push them out. The babies, like most fish, are ready to take care of themselves right away.

Tapeworm

1

A tapeworm can have as many as one million babies a day, and it has more sexual organs that any other creature on Earth. Basically, this parasite is one long chain of identical body segments that contain both male and female parts, each dedicated almost entirely to egg production. In fact, some scientists consider the segments as individuals in their own right and suggest that a tapeworm is really a colony! Each segment can make up to 40,000 eggs. Why so many?

Consider the life of a typical beef tapeworm: The eggs pass out through the host's feces (that's right: poop). Some of that fecal matter ends up in food for livestock like pigs or cows. It doesn't happen all the time (hence the need for so many eggs), but it happens enough. An animal eats the eggs, which hatch inside its gut. Then the larvae drill through the intestine into the bloodstream, which carries them to muscle tissue, where they form protective capsules and develop into a stage called bladder worm. When the animal is slaughtered for meat and served in raw or undercooked food, the bladder worm survives being eaten and attaches itself to the new host's intestine. There it develops into an adult tapeworm. So who is the new and final host? In this case, a person!

SPECIAL REPORT:
Love and Parasites

All life begins when boy meets girl, right? Not always. Many single-celled organisms simply divide to reproduce. Other organisms clone themselves. Clones are genetically identical offspring of the parent, whereas offspring of sexual parents have a variety of different genes. With each new individual, the deck is shuffled and new genes are dealt. This shuffling enables some individuals to fight off parasites that clones cannot. Scientists point to freshwater snails in Nigeria as evidence of this. These snails make clones except in cool weather, when they make males and females. The sexuals mature in the spring—just in time to fight off an annual parasite invasion. Coincidence? You decide. ●

Where's the beef?

CHAPTER 2 Family Matters

Parents will do just about anything for the sake of their children. Humans, however, aren't the only ones who will perform incredible feats for their offspring. From parents who protect their babies with tooth and claw to parents who give their kids the skin off their own back, we're counting down the most extreme stories of parenting in the animal kingdom.

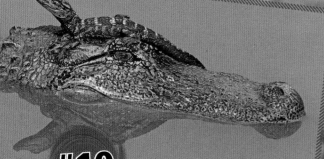

#10 Alligator

How does a cold-blooded gal make certain that her eggs stay warm when she can't regulate her own body heat? Alligator moms solve this problem by laying their eggs in a pile of rotting vegetation. The decaying material gives off enough heat to keep those eggs toasty warm. When the babies hatch, mom protects them for up to a year.

If the temperature in an alligator's nest is less than 88°F (31°C), all the babies will be female. If the nest temperature is higher than 91°F (32.7°C), all the babies will be male.

THAT'S WILD!

#9 Elephant

After being pregnant for 22 months, an elephant female gives birth to a baby weighing about 250 pounds—the biggest animal baby on land. But what's even more interesting is that elephant society is female-based. The grandmother is the leader of the herd, which consists of her daughters and granddaughters (males are forced out at around age 14). Since there are plenty of aunties to look after the youngsters, mom can eat more and make more milk for her baby, giving it a better shot at survival.

#8

Hornbill

Imagine being cooped up with hungry infants for months with only a tiny window to the outside. After a pair of hornbills find a hollow tree, the female seals herself inside with a special concrete made from her own dung and then lays her eggs. After incubating the eggs for about four weeks, she stays put to rear the chicks. Meanwhile, daddy hornbill is busy stuffing himself full of fruit and bringing it back (predigested) for mother and children.

Nice moves!

#7

Crane

There are 15 species of cranes, and all of them have elaborate courtship dances. Apparently, the activity helps females pump up the reproductive hormones that allow them to lay eggs. In 1976, George Archibald, a crane caregiver, put this notion to the test. Tex, a female whooping crane, had been hand-reared by humans and refused to accept a male crane as a mate. Scientists tried artificially implanting sperm, but Tex still couldn't produce eggs—that is, until Archibald began spending so much time with her, Tex allowed him to court her and began to dance with him!

#6

Southern Elephant Seal

At 1,700 pounds, the female southern elephant seal is no lightweight. However, you need to be big to have a baby in or near Antarctica. In fact, an elephant seal mom has to put on a couple of pounds a day so she can be ready to feed her infant when it's born. When the baby does arrive, it's got just one month to put on the blubber it needs to survive—while mom loses nearly a third of her body weight! After a month, she stops nursing it to mate and start the process over again.

Female elephant seals can spend 11 out of every 12 months being pregnant.

THAT'S WILD!

#5 Bitterling

When a male bitterling, a small freshwater fish, wants to mate, he first has to make friends with a mussel. He dances all around the shellfish to get it used to his presence so it won't "clam up" when he's around. Then he puts on a show for the local lady bitterlings. If one of them likes his look, she'll use her long egg tube to lay her eggs—inside the mussel! The male then fertilizes the eggs, and both parents leave. When the eggs hatch, the mussel spits out the hatchlings, but they don't leave without a souvenir: mussel larvae, which have attached themselves to the gills of the baby fish.

I asked you that before we left home.

#4 Emperor Penguin

When it comes to shared parenting, male and female emperor penguins take the prize. First, it takes huge energy resources to even make an egg in the frozen wastes of Antarctica. After laying, the female needs to refuel, so she passes the egg to the male for safekeeping—very, very carefully, so the egg won't touch the frozen ground and crack with cold, killing the chick inside. The male holds the egg on his feet, settling the skin of his brood pouch over it to keep it warm. Then he's on duty for about two months while the female goes off to forage. There's no protection from the ice and wind except for him and the other penguin dads. There's also no food. Meanwhile, chicks are hatching! What to feed those hungry mouths when you've had nothing to eat yourself? Dad spits up a special brew from his own stomach contents, and that keeps the baby happy until mom gets back with something more substantial—predigested fish!

#3 Marsupial Mouse

Pity the poor male marsupial mouse from Australia. These animal dads make babies so furiously that they die off shortly after mating! All the mating within a population happens at once, apparently triggered by lengthening days. And when the call to mate comes, the male gets so busy that he literally cannot do anything else. He can't eat, drink, or sleep—although since the mating frenzy usually lasts only about 12 hours, sleep isn't really an issue. Males rush from communal nest to communal nest, wooing as many females as possible. At the end, the males are completely done in. Stress hormones (and no food and water) combine to strip their bodies of proteins and fat, destroying their immune systems. All the males die within two weeks, leaving the pregnant females to raise their broods on their own.

During the mating frenzy, the females mate with so many males that babies in the same brood may have several different fathers.

THAT'S WILD!

You look familiar.

#2

Caecilian

Caecilians, a little-known type of amphibian, live underground in the tropics and come in a variety of sizes. The small ones are easily mistaken for worms, and the larger ones are often mistaken for snakes. Some caecilians lay eggs, while others give birth to live young. What makes some egg-laying East African species remarkably dedicated parents is the first meal a mom prepares for her hatchlings. Her body grows a thick nutrient-rich skin—which she then allows the hatchlings to rip off and eat! The babies have special teeth for the purpose, teeth that look an awful lot like the teeth used by live-born caecilians babies to get nutrition from their moms while they are still in the womb. Which all boils down to this: The babies that hatch and eat the skin off their mother's back may well be the missing link in the evolutionary chain between egg layers and live bearers.

- Caecilians range from just under 3 inches in length to more than 5 feet.
- The caecilian is the only vertebrate to have a retractable tentacle located on each side of its head that serves as a sensor in locating prey.

THAT'S WILD!

#1 Green Crab

The European green crab is a predatory shore crab that doesn't normally inspire pity. The exception is when it gets infected by *Sacculina carcini*, a parasitic barnacle. Then the green crab makes the ultimate parental sacrifice, and it's not even for her own children! In order to complete its life cycle and have offspring, the parasitic barnacle must hijack a host like the green crab and force it to do the hard labor of a mother barnacle.

During its free-swimming larval stage, a female *Sacculina* finds a crab, injects its cells into the crab's body, and takes its next form—a tiny slug-like creature, which basically takes over the crab's brain. From then on, the crab is the barnacle's tool, never having its own children, living only to serve its tenant. The *Sacculina* settles in the crab's underbelly and forms a knob.

When a male barnacle larva finds the crab, he injects *his* cells into the crab's body *and* into the female *Sacculina*. There he remains, continually fertilizing her eggs. The crab takes care of the knob—which fills with fresh parasite eggs every few weeks—the way she would her own brood. When the babies are ready to emerge, she helps them out with quick pulses of her body.

Not even male crabs are safe from the *Sacculina*. When a female barnacle larva finds a male crab, it forces the host to assume female behavior, caring for the parasitic barnacle's brood as he would never do if left to his own devices.

THAT'S WILD!

CHAPTER 3 Survival of the Fittest

You have to have some pretty intense skills to survive all the curveballs that nature can throw at you. Some animals have become experts at the art of camouflage (blending in with one's surroundings) in order to avoid unpleasant, even fatal, confrontations. Others have become skillful at surviving harsh environments. Still others have put all their energy into finding ways to actively fight off predation. Let's meet ten of the most extreme masters of the art of survival.

#9

Leafy Sea Dragon

The leafy sea dragon, a cousin of the seahorse, grows long, leaf-like projections all over its body in order to blend in with its surroundings. Powered slowly through the water by small, nearly transparent fins on its back, the sea dragon looks like nothing more than a floating piece of seaweed.

#10

Arctic Fox

The arctic fox, a champion survivor of the long polar winters, has some of the densest, warmest fur in the mammal world. But the true secret to its survival success is the color-changing ability of its fur. In winter, when food is scarce, the arctic fox often gets by on leftovers from a polar bear's kill. The tricky part is not getting eaten by the polar bear. So the fox changes the color of its coat to a pure white that blends in with the ice and snow, allowing it to hide in plain sight and escape the bear's notice.

Like a seahorse, a male sea dragon gives birth to babies. For protection, he transplants a bit of real seaweed to his body to hide the brood patch under his tail.

THAT'S WILD!

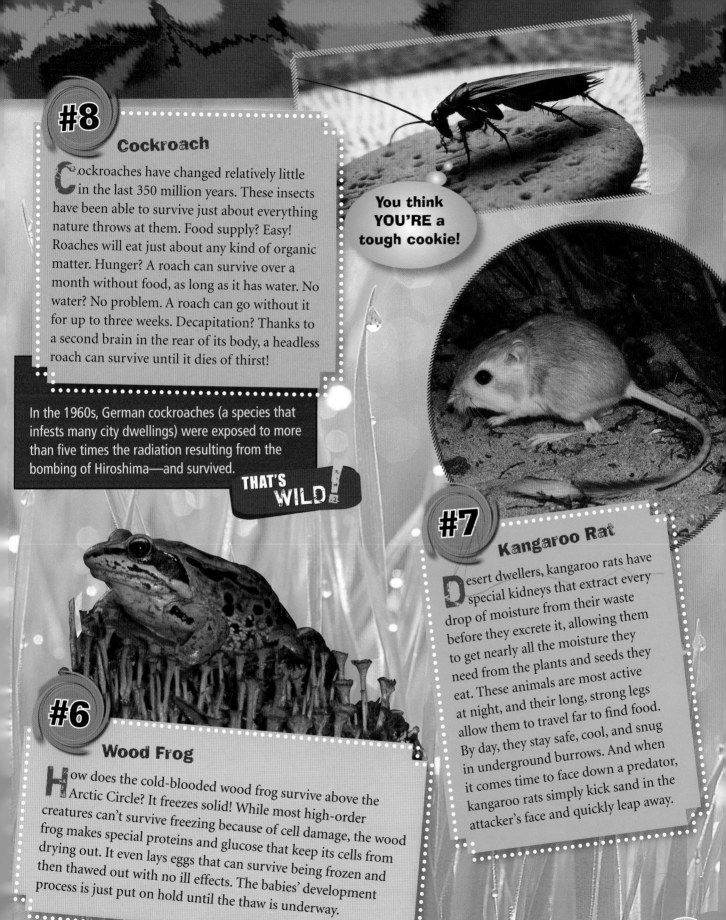

#8

Cockroach

Cockroaches have changed relatively little in the last 350 million years. These insects have been able to survive just about everything nature throws at them. Food supply? Easy! Roaches will eat just about any kind of organic matter. Hunger? A roach can survive over a month without food, as long as it has water. No water? No problem. A roach can go without it for up to three weeks. Decapitation? Thanks to a second brain in the rear of its body, a headless roach can survive until it dies of thirst!

In the 1960s, German cockroaches (a species that infests many city dwellings) were exposed to more than five times the radiation resulting from the bombing of Hiroshima—and survived.

You think YOU'RE a tough cookie!

THAT'S WILD!

#7

Kangaroo Rat

Desert dwellers, kangaroo rats have special kidneys that extract every drop of moisture from their waste before they excrete it, allowing them to get nearly all the moisture they need from the plants and seeds they eat. These animals are most active at night, and their long, strong legs allow them to travel far to find food. By day, they stay safe, cool, and snug in underground burrows. And when it comes time to face down a predator, kangaroo rats simply kick sand in the attacker's face and quickly leap away.

#6

Wood Frog

How does the cold-blooded wood frog survive above the Arctic Circle? It freezes solid! While most high-order creatures can't survive freezing because of cell damage, the wood frog makes special proteins and glucose that keep its cells from drying out. It even lays eggs that can survive being frozen and then thawed out with no ill effects. The babies' development process is just put on hold until the thaw is underway.

#5

Hoatzin

In the tropical rain forests of South America there lives a bird that can digest even the toughest plant foods. The hoatzin has a colony of bacteria in its crop (an enlarged pouch near the throat) that ferments the leaves, breaking them down into digestible material. Because the hoatzin has an enlarged crop to store the bacteria, it's rather clumsy, so it can take young birds a while to master flying. To compensate, the young birds have an extra set of claws on their wings that they use to climb the branches of trees and escape predators. When that doesn't work, they jump into the water below the nest and swim to safety.

Because of its fermentation process, the hoatzin smells really bad. In fact, one of its nicknames is "stinkbird."

THAT'S WILD!

#4

Camouflage Crab

Sometimes the survival skill of choice is hiding. It's often the best way to avoid confrontations with unpleasant predators with dinner on their mind. Spider crabs use their claws to clip bits of plants or sponges and affix them to the tiny hairs on their shells. It's no wonder crabs from this family are called camouflage crabs, or decorator crabs. The best part is that their disguise is totally changeable! When a crab moves to a new environment, it can redecorate itself with local materials to blend in with its new surroundings.

Some spider crabs gently rock back and forth so the seaweed planted on their shells sways naturally.

THAT'S WILD!

#3

Camel

For centuries, people have relied on camels, the "ships of the desert," to help them travel in unforgiving territory. Both the two-humped Bactrian camels of Central Asia and the one-humped dromedaries of Saharan Africa are perfectly adapted to their desert lives. They can go for a week without food and walk up to a hundred miles without water, thanks to the portable pantries they carry on their backs. While the humps don't store water, they do store huge fat reserves. If food or water isn't available, camels can turn to their fat reserves, which their body breaks down into water and energy. And when they do get the chance to drink up after a dry spell, camels can suck up 30 gallons in 13 minutes—a rate that would kill other creatures.

The camel's other desert adaptations include large, padlike feet that provide plenty of surface area to help them balance on soft, shifting sand; an extra set of long eyelashes that keep their eyes free from sand and grit; and nostrils they can close to keep nasal passages clear during a sandstorm.

I feel like I'm in Camelot!

Camel milk is incredibly nutritious. It's low in cholesterol, contains triple the amount of vitamin C found in cow's milk, and keeps for up to four months when refrigerated.

THAT'S WILD!

#2

Caterpillars

The soft-bodied larvae of moths and butterflies have evolved some incredible survival skills. When you are basically a big, fat, juicy meal on a leafy plate, you either develop defensive skills or you're dead meat.

Some caterpillars, like the monarch butterfly, eat the tough, bitter leaves of plants that make unpleasant-tasting chemicals that they store in their body and use for their own defense. Predators learn to recognize and stay away from these caterpillars with their vivid, warning colors of red, yellow, and black.

Other caterpillars have developed protective coloration to fool predators. For example, the red-spotted purple butterfly caterpillar resembles bird droppings, while the tiger swallowtail butterfly larva has markings that look like large eyes to scare predators away. A hawk moth caterpillar mimics a snake to frighten its enemies.

Still other caterpillars have the ability to exude foul odors or grow irritating hairs or bristles with barbed tips that lodge in the throats of predators. Some larvae, such as the spiny oak slug moth, even have stinging hairs.

The caterpillar of a South American silk moth makes a chemical that keeps blood from clotting and can cause a human to bleed to death.

THAT'S WILD!

SPECIAL REPORT:
Reverse Camouflage

The parasitic fluke that is called *Leucochloridium paradoxum* is a type of flatworm that needs two different hosts to survive. The final host is a bird, and the first host is an amber snail. The snail eats the eggs of the flatworm, which are excreted by a bird. Once the snail is infected, the parasite crawls into the snail's tentacles, which are often transparent to allow the creature to avoid notice by predators. The stripy flukes can be seen through the tentacles and they mimic caterpillars—a bird's favorite food! So in this case, the flatworm is an organism that camouflages itself to look like another in order to get eaten! •

#1 Giant Tubeworm

The ocean floor at the deepest depths gets no sunlight, so the water is icy cold and the pressure is unbelievable. Scientists once thought nothing could live there, but they were wrong. In 1977, they discovered geysers on the ocean floor they called hydrothermal vents—and the amazing organisms that live near them.

Studies revealed that these organisms survive by chemosynthesis, the conversion of chemicals into energy. Bacteria are the basis of this food chain, and colonies of them were found to live inside giant tubeworms. These creatures consist of a 9-foot-tall, tough outer tube made of chitin (the same material that makes up the outer shells of insects) with large red plumes shooting out of their tops. They have no mouth, eyes, or stomach. So how do they eat?

During their free-swimming larval stage, the worms do have a mouth. Larval worms swim around until they find a thermal vent, then plant themselves near the crack and suck up bacteria that live off the hydrogen sulfide spewed out by the vents along with other minerals and gases. The worms store the bacteria inside their body and collect hydrogen sulfide through their plumes. In return, the bacteria convert the hydrogen sulfide into food for the worms. As the worms grow, the mouth, which is no longer needed, disappears.

The Pompeii worm, also found near hydrothermal vents, can live in temperatures up to 194°F (90°C), which would kill any other known animal.

THAT'S WILD!

Like my giant tube top?

4 Pick Your Poison

When is poison not really poison? When it is venom. Although we use these words almost interchangeably, there are slight differences in meaning. Poison is the more general term: It's a substance that causes injury or death by chemical means. It can be introduced through the skin or by ingestion. Venom, on the other hand, must be injected, and that involves a bite or a sting. Here are ten of the most extremely poisonous creatures on Earth.

#10

Shrew

Because the shrew has a furiously fast metabolism, it has to kill and eat at least its own weight in food every day. How does it manage that feat? It has poisonous saliva that can paralyze prey much larger than itself (but not as large as a human). The paralyzed prey can stay alive for a few days, so the shrew can stash food for future use.

An excited shrew's heart beats 1,200 times per minute—more than seven times faster than a hardworking human's.

THAT'S WILD!

#9

Gila Monster

It may be called "monster," but the Gila monster isn't very monster-like. This lizard uses its venom mainly in self-defense. It has a deadly bite, grabbing hold with an unshakeable grip and razor-sharp teeth that slash. Its poisonous saliva runs down grooves in its teeth and drips into the wounds. The more the Gila monster chews, the more poison is delivered.

#8
Stingray

What shark relative causes 50 times more injuries in people than sharks? Stingrays! That's because these shallows-dwellers like to bury themselves in the sandy sea floor. If you stand on one, watch out! The whiplike tail zings out, giving you a quick slap on the leg or foot—along with a good dose of venom from a barbed spine. The venom contains flesh-eating enzymes that make even big predators, like orcas (killer whales), think twice about eating stingrays—and that's the whole idea.

What's your sign?

#7
Scorpion

In Mexico, scorpions are blamed for about 1,000 human deaths per year. Luckily for humans, the stings of most scorpions have venom that is deadly only to other arthropods. Scientists are learning that scorpions may also be able to choose whether to go for the kill or simply a knockout punch. Apparently, it takes far more energy to make that special cocktail of proteins that kills.

Scorpions glow in the dark when exposed to ultraviolet light.

THAT'S WILD!

#6
Cane Toad

Hands off this big fellow! The cane toad, a chunky amphibian from Central and South America, has large poison glands behind its eyes and across its back. When it's threatened, the toad exudes a milky toxin that is deadly to many animals and even to people when absorbed through mucous membranes like the eyes, nose, and mouth. If handled roughly, the toads can spray the toxin for a short distance.

Cane toads were imported by many countries to control sugar cane pests, but the toads have few natural predators in their new homes and have been so successful, they have become pests themselves.

THAT'S WILD!

#5

Sea Krait

When a sea krait, a type of sea snake found in Southeast Asia and the Pacific Islands, starts to weave rapidly through the water, it creates a useful optical illusion. The snake looks like it's moving in the opposite direction from where it's really heading. That means a predator could be tricked into attacking the wrong end of the snake, allowing it to escape relatively unharmed. Even though the sea krait has some of the most potent snake venom in the world—one drop can kill three adult humans—it is one of those animals that would rather not fight. It only bites when provoked, saving its venom for hunting and only occasionally using it for self-defense.

A sea snake has only one lung, but it's nearly as long as its body. It can also get oxygen through its skin, diffused from seawater.

THAT'S WILD!

- Funnel-web venom is more dangerous to people than to cats and dogs.
- The Sydney funnel-web spider bites hard! A fang can actually pierce a fingernail.

THAT'S WILD!

#4

Sydney Funnel-web Spider

Meet the Sydney funnel-web spider of Australia. It's one of the most venomous spiders in the world—some say it's the most venomous. It's certainly an extremely aggressive spider. How does an animal that spends most of its life in an underground burrow get such a bad rep? Males leave their burrows to find mates, and as many of them as possible, since they die shortly after reaching maturity. This wanderlust carries them into people's houses and garages. Males also have an extra chemical in their venom that makes their bite even more potent than the females'—an unusual feature in spiders.

Blue-ringed Octopus

You can look, but you'd better not touch! Because by the time you see the bright blue rings on a blue-ringed octopus (which is normally brown when calm), it's ready to attack. This usually shy, golf-ball sized creature packs a venomous double-punch. It's got one kind of venom for its prey (crabs, mostly) and another, super-deadly one for fighting off predators. One tiny bite from this octopus can paralyze 20 people, stopping their ability to breathe. There is no antidote for the venom. Victims need artificial respiration and time to outlast the venom's effects.

I'll ring you later.

Blue-ringed octopi don't make their own venom. They use bacteria in their salivary glands to do the dirty work.

THAT'S WILD!

SPECIAL REPORT:
Octopus IQ

Smart mollusks? You bet! Octopi are among the most intelligent of invertebrates. Their central nervous system is big and complex. It has to be, say scientists. Octopi don't live very long (even the largest live only three or four years), and their parents don't stick around to show them the score. And they have a huge amount to learn, like how to hunt, how to protect themselves, how to control their changeable coloration, and how to coordinate and synthesize all the data collected by the sensory organs on their tentacles and suckers. Giant Pacific octopi are known to be able to solve complex puzzles and open jar lids to retrieve treats. •

Cone Shell

This tropical snail may look like a slowpoke, but it stabs with extreme speed. And the venom it injects works even faster. When a United States Marine based in Guam posed for a photo with two cone shells and both struck him in the neck, he died just four seconds later. It turns out cone shell venom is a cocktail of 50 to 100 different chemical components. Scientists studying these components think they could produce scores of powerful painkillers plus drugs to treat mental illness and disorders like epilepsy. One particular painkiller may be 1,000 times more effective than morphine, but without the side effects.

Most of the research is done on dead cone shells, and, unfortunately, they are fast becoming an endangered species because their beautiful shells are so highly prized by collectors. However, some scientists believe that there's a big future in cone shell farming. In other words, "milking" live cone shells for their venom. It's a hazardous job, but it's already afforded surprise benefits. For instance, it's been discovered that the milked venom contains extra enzymes not present in venom from dead cone shells. And it turns out that venom milked at different times contains slightly different chemicals.

One scoop or two?

#1 Box Jellyfish

What is it about Australia? Between its waters and its countryside, it supports some of the most venomous creatures on Earth! But no venomous creature can clear an entire beach as quickly as the box jellyfish, also known as the sea wasp. This nearly transparent sea monster has sixty 8-foot-long trailing tentacles covered with 4 billion stinging cells. The slightest touch means those cells will blast you with quick shots of a powerful neurotoxin, which acts on the nervous system. It has to be fast and powerful, because otherwise the jellyfish might lose a delicate tentacle during the death throes of its prey.

Box jellyfish are plentiful in the warm Australian waters during the summer months of November to about April. No one knows where the jellyfish go during the Australian winter, but researchers have discovered that individuals sleep on the ocean floor from mid-afternoon to dawn during the summer.

Today, Australian lifeguards wear Lycra suits to protect them from box jellyfish stings. But they used to wear pantyhose, which were thick enough to prevent stings while lightweight enough to be comfortable.

THAT'S WILD!

CHAPTER 5 Don't Mess with Us!

Sometimes you have to fight for what you want. It can be for any number of reasons: room, food, or even a friend or mate. Animals are like that, too. In fact, some animals seem to be hard-wired to fight, and they'll get into it with any creature that's in their way. Others are shy and will only fight animals like themselves. Meet ten of the most extremely bad-tempered animals around, starting with a little fish that has an attitude problem and ending with a mighty beast that no one dares to cross.

#9 Chameleon

These lizards are famous for their ability to almost instantly change their coloration to match their surroundings. Too bad it's not quite true. Chameleons can change color, all right. But the change indicates how they're feeling, not camouflage. When one of these solitary animals meets up with another of its kind, they'll both turn red with anger in 30 seconds. A burst of colors means the animal is excited; green/yellow indicates calm; and black/brown indicates one stressed-out chameleon.

#10 Siamese Fighting Fish

The top fighter in the fish world is actually a popular aquarium fish. As long as it's with fish of other species, the male Siamese fighting fish is safe and easy to keep. But put it in a tank with another of its kind and watch out. Chalk its behavior up to male dominance. There can be a big pond with only two of these fish present, but they'll still fight each other to the death.

In Thailand, watching and betting on Siamese fighting fish was once a popular sport.

THAT'S WILD!

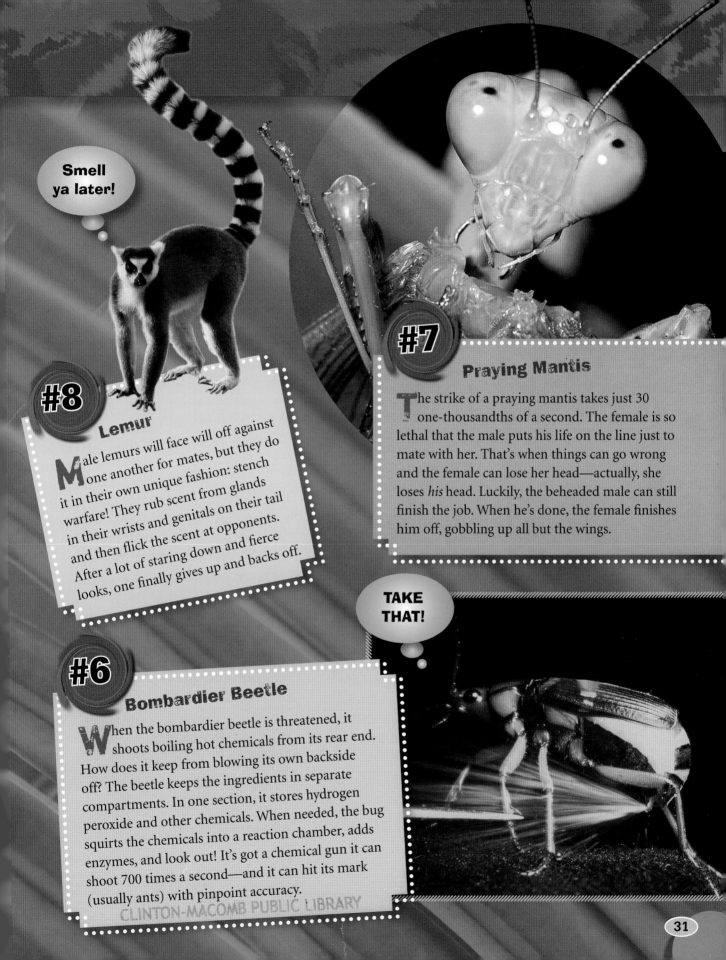

Smell ya later!

#8

Lemur

Male lemurs will face will off against one another for mates, but they do it in their own unique fashion: stench warfare! They rub scent from glands in their wrists and genitals on their tail and then flick the scent at opponents. After a lot of staring down and fierce looks, one finally gives up and backs off.

#7

Praying Mantis

The strike of a praying mantis takes just 30 one-thousandths of a second. The female is so lethal that the male puts his life on the line just to mate with her. That's when things can go wrong and the female can lose her head—actually, she loses *his* head. Luckily, the beheaded male can still finish the job. When he's done, the female finishes him off, gobbling up all but the wings.

TAKE THAT!

#6

Bombardier Beetle

When the bombardier beetle is threatened, it shoots boiling hot chemicals from its rear end. How does it keep from blowing its own backside off? The beetle keeps the ingredients in separate compartments. In one section, it stores hydrogen peroxide and other chemicals. When needed, the bug squirts the chemicals into a reaction chamber, adds enzymes, and look out! It's got a chemical gun it can shoot 700 times a second—and it can hit its mark (usually ants) with pinpoint accuracy.

#5 Tasmanian Devil

The Tasmanian devil is one of those creatures that is hard-wired to have tantrums. It starts at birth. The mother can have as many as 20 babies, but she's only got enough teats for four—two pairs and no spares—so it's a fight to the finish. The ones that don't make it get eaten by mom. The surviving joeys bite and tussle all the time, which finally drives the mother out of the den. By this time, the little devils are hardened fighters and fully prepared for adulthood. They are ready to fight rival devils for food and mates.

SPECIAL REPORT:
When Bad Things Happen to Good Biters

In the late 1990s, a wildlife photographer noticed a Tasmanian devil with a facial tumor. Since then, the disease has spread rapidly, pushing the devils' teeth out of line and making it difficult for the animals to eat, finally resulting in their starving to death. Scientists think the tumors are caused by cancer cells that get transmitted during mating fights. Tasmanian devils are so genetically similar, the cancer cells may not be recognized as foreign by the animals' own immune system. Many wildlife conservation organizations are discussing the possibility of beginning captive breeding programs in case the wild population gets wiped out. •

#4 Honey Badger

You have to be pretty crazy to take on a leopard in a fight over food, but that's the honey badger for you. It screams in anger, rattles its teeth, and even throws stink bombs from its anal glands. It loves honey so much that it will risk the stinging power of an entire nest of honeybees—the aggressive African ones—to get to the sweet stuff. This fearless animal, or ratel, as it is called in Afrikaans, has even developed a special relationship with the honeyguide bird. The bird leads the ratel to a hive and lets it do the hard work of breaking into the nest. After the ratel has had its fill of honey, the bird feasts on the larvae, wax, and leftover honey.

Show me the honey!

Ratels hunt snakes for food and can even shake off the deadly venom of puff adders! **THAT'S WILD!**

Rhinoceros

It may be a plant eater, but you don't want to mess with a rhinoceros. This big, grumpy herbivore has excellent hearing and a finely tuned sense of smell, but it has poor eyesight, which is probably why it charges anything—including butterflies—at the least provocation. Rhinos in India and Nepal have caused more human deaths than tigers and leopards. Rhinos have even been known to attack working elephants.

The five surviving species of rhinoceros are known for the large horn positioned on their forehead (some species have a second horn as well). Oddly enough, the horn is actually made of compressed hairs of keratin, the same material as fingernails. Scientists don't precisely know why the rhino even has a horn, because a de-horned animal appears to function just fine without it.

Outa my way!

- Rhinos can gallop up to about 30 miles per hour.
- Ground rhino horn is an important ingredient in many traditional Asian medicines, and the trade in illegal rhino parts endangers populations of all the species. A hunter can get thousands of dollars for a single horn.

THAT'S WILD!

Now all I need is a bagel!

#2

Bear

Whoever came up with the notion that bears are cute and cuddly didn't know much about real bears. These animals are often the biggest and most dangerous mammals around. Male bears are ferocious and will even go after bear cubs. Luckily for the cubs, mama bear usually isn't far off—and no one can say, "Don't mess with me!" quite as effectively as a mother bear protecting her cubs.

Bears need large territories because it takes a lot of land to support enough food—including eggs, fish, deer, fruit, nuts, ants, bees, and honey—to feed them. A male will allow some females into his territory (after all, they are smaller and don't eat as much), but they generally won't tolerate other males. They need to conserve every ounce of energy for the long, hard winter ahead when they'll have to live off fat stores, and confrontations with other males simply use up too much energy. So how do they minimize such confrontations? They rely on scent marking to tell other bears, "Stay away—or else!"

When Vikings put on a bearskin (called a *bear-sark*) during battle, they believed they could magically assume the fighting powers of a bear. Indeed, Vikings who wore these skins did put up a frenzy of a fight. In fact, *bear-sark* is the origin of the English word "berserk."

THAT'S WILD!

#1 ★ Lion

The strongest male lions usually have the best manes, because mane growth is controlled by the male hormone, testosterone. And the more a male has, the more aggressive he's likely to be.

THAT'S WILD!

Even though a lion isn't really "the king of the jungle" (lions don't live in the jungle—they live in open grasslands called savannas), a male lion is king of his domain. The pride may be established and held together by the breeding females (who are related), but it's the males who rule. A strong male can keep control of his pride (or keep other males out) for about two to three years, which is long enough for at least one generation of his cubs to grow to maturity.

When a young male takes over a pride from an older male, he'll kill all the cubs. That's because females who lose their cubs will come back into season within two or three weeks, which means that the new head of the pride can start making his own babies sooner. If a lioness tries to defend her cub from the winning male, she may lose her life.

Male lions are extremely strong. One swipe from a lion's paw can break a zebra's back. But the very feature that distinguishes a male—his mane—prevents him from being the best hunter. Lions need stealth to hunt their prey, and males are simply too showy to hide well. Instead, the lionesses do most of the hunting.

Go ahead– make my day!

CHAPTER 6 Animal Olympians

It takes guts, talent, and good muscles to make a great athlete. Humans have taken a body that's okay for doing lots of different things and used ingenuity and a bit of technology to shape it into a performance machine. Animals, however, have been driven by the need to survive—in unique habitats, under unique conditions—to develop some truly amazing athletic skills, and all without help from technology. Get ready to count down ten of the most extreme animal athletes in the world.

#9

Gannet: Diving

These large seabirds dive for fish from heights of up to 100 feet, reaching speeds of about 60 miles per hour, which allows them to go deeper than most seabirds. How do they keep from being killed when they hit the water? Special air sacs in their face and chest inflate on impact to cushion the blow. Though underwater for only about ten seconds, these birds can catch and swallow their prey before they get back to the surface.

#10

Gibbon: Gymnastics

Gibbons take the prize for being the most graceful and athletic gymnasts, swinging with ease through the upper canopy of tropical rain forests in China, India, Indonesia, and Malaysia. With long, loose arms and even longer fingers, these small apes have adapted superbly to their special habitat. Their wrists have a ball and socket joint that moves freely in more than one direction, which reduces stress on the shoulder joint and minimizes the energy the gibbons need to swing through the trees.

#8
Elephant Shrew: 400-meter Run

The elephant shrew is both a fast runner and a good jumper—it has to be, or it could never avoid its predators, mostly snakes and birds of prey. Often referred to by its Bantu name, sengi, to distinguish it from rodents and true shrews, this animal has a long, mobile nose for sniffing out insect prey. It uses its long hind legs to jump from branch to branch—sometimes leaping up to 3 feet.

#7
Cheetah: 100-meter Dash

The fastest mammal on land, the cheetah is long, lean, and built for speed. Its semi-retractable claws give it extra traction, while its long tail helps it balance when making hairpin turns. It also has a flexible spine, oversized liver, an enlarged heart, extra lung capacity, and big nostrils to cool that air—special features that allow it to reach speeds of up to 70 miles per hour, though only for about 100 yards. A cheetah can go from zero to 60 miles per hour in under four seconds.

Cheetahs are so genetically similar that skin grafts from unrelated animals are not rejected as foreign tissue.

THAT'S WILD!

#6
Silver-spotted Skipper Caterpillar: Shot Put

The caterpillars of the silver-spotted skipper butterfly fire pellets of poop up to 5 feet—about the same as a human spitting a watermelon seed a distance of 230 feet. Once a caterpillar ejects a pellet onto an anal plate, blood pressure builds up beneath it until it's high enough to move the plate, flinging the pellet away. This behavior may have developed to keep parasitic wasps from locating it by smelling its feces. Were that to happen, the wasp would inject its eggs into the caterpillar—which would hatch and eat the living caterpillar from the inside out!

#5 Kangaroo: Long Jump

Australia's kangaroos are expert long jumpers, covering 40 feet in a single bound and reaching speeds of about 30 miles per hour when they really get hopping. And the faster a kangaroo travels, the more energy efficient it gets. Unlike humans, who tend to increase their number of strides to go faster, kangaroos save energy by simply lengthening their stride. When kangaroos move on land, they are unable to move their hind legs separately (even though they can do so while swimming).

Peace and love, my brother.

Legend has it that when westerners first landed in Australia and asked the locals what the funny-looking hopping animals were called, they were told, "Kangaroo." Translated from the Aboriginal, that means, "I don't understand your question."

THAT'S WILD!

#4 Gorilla: Weight Lifting

They may look big and scary, but gorillas are actually peaceful, shy plant-eaters that don't even fight among themselves when it comes to finding food. Instead, they eat easily available plant material (and occasionally some insects), using their great strength to uproot trees and other plants with tender shoots, or to break open woody plants to get to the edible pith inside. And it takes quite a set of muscles to do that kind of work!

- All the captive gorillas in zoos are lowland gorillas; mountain gorillas die in captivity.
- Male gorillas can eat 75 pounds of food a day and females, up to 40 pounds.

THAT'S WILD!

#3
Klipspringer: High Jump

This dainty little creature (it stands only 22 inches high at the shoulder) is the ballet dancer of the antelope world. All hoofed animals can be said to walk on their tiptoes, but a klipspringer walks and stands on the *tips* of its tiptoes (imagine standing on the edges of your toenails instead of your toes). This feat allows the klipspringer to stand on an area so small that no other animal could balance there. And that is the special secret of the klipspringer's success: It can jump 15 times its own height straight up a cliff to escape a predator, land on a shelf the size of a quarter, and stick the landing without any trouble.

The klipspringer has many features similar to a mountain goat's, even though the two are not closely related. In the middle of each split hoof, a klipspringer has a fleshy area that allows it to grip rocky surfaces. Tan fur speckled with gray, white, and black helps it disappear into the background.

- When klipspringers stand still, they bring their front and hind legs together, something other antelope can't do.
- Klipspringers have scent glands in the corners of their eyes that they use for marking territory.

THAT'S WILD!

Sailfish: Swimming

Everything about the sailfish is fast, fast, fast! Sometimes called billfish for the long, pointy beak or bill on the upper jaw, sailfish have been clocked at 68 miles per hour. But that's not the only speedy aspect of this fish's life. After a female sailfish lays her eggs, the babies are ready to hatch in just 36 hours! The hatchlings have a race of their own—they do most of their growing in their first year or two of life, growing from 0.12 inch at hatching to around 5 feet by the end of year one. Fully-grown adults are around 6 to 7 feet long.

Sailfish swim long distances far from shore, so they are difficult for scientists to tag and track. Little is known about them except that they swim in the tropical and subtropical waters of all the major oceans. Sport fishers have reported seeing sailfish cooperate to hunt, using their high dorsal (top) fins to herd prey—like tuna, mackerel, and squid. Sailfish tend to keep their dorsal fins retracted when moving fast, leaping in and out of the water.

- The biggest sailfish ever caught weighed 141 pounds and was over 10 feet long.
- Female sailfish can lay nearly 5 million eggs during one spawning.

THAT'S WILD!

#1 Sooty Shearwater: Marathon

For years, scientists thought that the arctic tern made the longest migration, traveling from the North Pole to the South Pole and back again. However, the arctic tern is too small to carry an electronic tag, so it's never been tracked and no one knows exactly how far it flies or whether it makes the roundtrip in a single season.

In August 2006, researchers tracking another seabird, the sooty shearwater, announced that three of the tagged birds had flown from their breeding grounds in New Zealand across the Pacific Ocean to the coast of Chile, re-crossed the ocean to Japan, and finally returned to New Zealand—a distance of 40,000 miles—in just 200 days!

For now, the sooty shearwater holds the record for longest migration, but perhaps that will change should scientists find a way to track the arctic tern electronically. Only time—and advances in technology—will tell.

I'm on the right track!

- Sooty shearwaters spend most of their life at sea, coming ashore only to breed.
- A sooty shearwater can dive into the sea up to 225 feet deep in pursuit of prey.

THAT'S WILD

7 Stranger Than Fiction

The creature world abounds with weird-looking body parts. For the most part, though, they serve useful purposes for the animals that possess them. Sometimes creatures have these adaptations for self-protection. Sometimes the adaptations make the animals more efficient at finding food. Sometimes they are what the females of the species find the most attractive. Here are ten of the most extreme-looking creatures you'll ever see.

#9

Narwhal

The narwhal, which belongs to the family of toothed whales, usually has only one tooth—but it's a doozy! It grows right through the flesh of the upper lip into a long spiral tusk, sometimes as long as 10 feet. Until recently, scientists didn't know what to make of the tusks. Recent discoveries made by a dentist, however, indicate that they may be a sensory organ that tells a narwhal almost everything it needs to know about seawater, such as salinity and water pressure.

#10

Proboscis Monkey

Proboscis monkeys get their name from the big nose sported by the males. Scientists aren't sure why the monkeys have them. One thought is that the noses might serve to amplify the sound of the monkeys' calls in the forest. However, most experts think that it's a beauty thing. Females don't have them, and the ladies tend to favor the males with the biggest honkers.

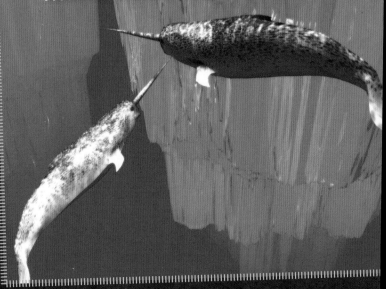

#8

Aye-aye

Is there an animal with the face of a rodent, the body of a monkey, the tail of a squirrel, and ears like a bat? Aye-aye, sir! No, that's not a sailor's word for "yes." It's a type of lemur called an aye-aye, the only primate in the world to use echolocation (using sound to find things). The aye-aye taps on branches with its long bony middle finger. Then it listens for the difference in sound between solid wood and tunnels filled with tasty grubs. Once food is detected, the aye-aye breaks the wood open with its strong, sharp teeth and uses its long finger to pick out the bugs.

#7

Jacana

The amazing, lily-trotting jacana has toes and claws so long that they equal 60 percent of its total body length! By spreading its body weight over such a large area, this incredible bird can actually tiptoe across floating vegetation, using its toes to turn over leaves in search of fish and insects. Some people swear they've seen the jacana walk across water!

Unlike most kinds of birds, the larger, more colorful female jacanas compete for mates while the dads build the nest, incubate the eggs, and rear the chicks.

THAT'S WILD!

#6

Giraffe

Everything about the giraffe—the world's tallest animal—is built on a large scale. It stands up to 17 feet tall from hoofs to horn tips. Its legs alone are taller than the average man, and it's got a 6-foot long neck. The giraffe's extreme height and 20-inch-long tongue allow it to eat leaves no other animal can reach, but it's had to make some serious adaptations to reach these heights. The vertebrae in its neck are each as long as 10 inches. It has an extra large heart to pump blood all the way up the neck, and special valves to manage the flow. Otherwise, a giraffe might faint from lack of oxygen.

In mating battles, male giraffes whip their necks and use their heads like sledgehammers. This behavior is called "necking."

THAT'S WILD!

#5

Babirusa

With extraordinary curlicue tusks that burst through the top of its snout, the babirusa looks pretty extreme. A nearly hairless member of the pig family that's found only on certain islands in Indonesia, the babirusa (which means "pig-deer") doesn't use its snout to root for food. Both male and female babirusas have tusks that protrude from the lower jaw, but only the male sports the fantastic teeth that grow out of the nose and curve back over the eyes. Experts suggest that these tusks protect the animal's eyes during mating battles.

- The sloth spends so much time hanging upside down that some of its internal organs (like the liver and pancreas) have turned upside down in comparison to other mammals.
- Sloths can hang on to branches so tightly that even after they're dead they remain securely in place!

THAT'S WILD!

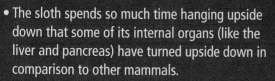

#4

Sloth

A sloth eats mostly leaves, which can be very hard to digest, so it has developed extra stomach chambers to process the food slowly, with special gut bacteria to break it down. It eats, moves (incredibly slowly), sleeps, and mates while hanging upside down from big, hook-shaped claws. In fact, the sloth is so well suited to hanging in trees that it can't really walk on the ground. But what's even stranger are the plants growing in its long fur! A special groove in each strand allows algae to take root, so the sloth ends up looking like a large hanging plant!

SPECIAL REPORT:
Adaptations Gone Wild!

Several species of insects and mites have adapted themselves exclusively to living on sloths. Many of the invaders wait for the sloth to make its weekly descent from the trees. Then, while the sloth digs a shallow hole in the dirt, does its business, and covers the waste with leaves, the freeloaders hop off, grab a snack from the feces or lay their eggs in it, and then hop back on. One species of moth breaks off its wings and lives the rest of its life on the sloth! •

SPECIAL REPORT:
Attack of the Mutant Frogs!

Frogs absorb pollutants through their lungs and through their skin, so they respond quickly to increased pollution. Because of this, frogs are considered an "indicator species" for the environment, something like the canaries that were used to test the air quality in mines. In recent years, some frog species have disappeared altogether. In other species, the males are losing their ability to breed. Some frogs have physical deformities, like extra or missing limbs.

In the case of the multi-legged frogs, a parasitic flatworm causes extra limbs to form. However, the fact that so many multi-legged frogs have appeared in recent years leads scientists to believe that fertilizer runoff is increasing the flatworm population, exposing more frogs to more parasites. •

#3
Hairy Frog

Okay, so I'm a bald hairy frog. What's it to ya?

When naturalist Gerald Durrell was collecting animals for European zoos in the late 1940s, he was the first person to bring back what was considered one of the most remarkable amphibians in the world: the African hairy frog. This animal had been mentioned in textbooks, but most people doubted that it really existed. After all, a frog with hair? Even many of the locals in Cameroon, home of the hairy frog, said there was no such animal. Clearly, they were wrong. The hairy frog does exist, but the hairs are actually fine filaments of skin. Only the male has these "hairs," and he only develops them during breeding season.

Being amphibians that are comfortable in water and on land, frogs have two different ways to take in oxygen. On land, they use lungs to breathe. But in water, frogs absorb oxygen right through their skin. Having lots of extra skin allows the hairy frog to stay underwater for longer periods just when he needs it most—when he's guarding his mate's fertilized eggs.

- The Aboriginals, native people of Australia, thought the platypus was the child of a union between a duck and a water rat.
- The platypus shares so many traits with birds and reptiles that scientists hope to study it further to find more links among them.
- On land, the platypus has to crawl about on its knuckles because of the webbing between its toes.

THAT'S WILD!

#2

Platypus

With the rounded bill of a duck, the flat paddle feet and body of a beaver, poisonous spurs on its hind legs (male), and the ability to lay eggs (female), the platypus is the Frankenstein of the animal world. The 18th-century scientists who first examined this Australian mammal thought it was a hoax and looked for evidence that it was really a collection of sewn-together body parts. Actually, this strange creature has existed in its current form for about 100,000 years and is sometimes called a living fossil.

The platypus has a number of other, not so obvious, features that make it unique among mammals. It has venom that it injects with its ankle spurs during fierce mating battles. The venom isn't lethal to humans, but it does cause severe pain. The platypus also has special receptors in its bill that allow it to sense the electric impulses given off by living creatures when they move or breathe. When it hunts, it closes its eyes and roots around with its bill, relying completely on its electrosense to locate prey such as worms and shellfish.

#1 Deep-sea Anglerfish

The deep-sea anglerfish has a built-in lure that sprouts from its forehead and glows in the dark, thanks to colonies of bioluminescent bacteria that live inside the fish. The anglerfish wiggles this handy lure to attract prey, which can be twice as big as it is. It has huge jaws, which can stretch to swallow large fish, and lots of sharp teeth.

But the really weird body part of an anglerfish is the male. When scientists first began studying certain kinds of anglerfish, they noticed that they only captured females. Then they noticed a strange little growth on the females. That growth turned out to be what was left of the male anglerfish!

In some kinds of anglerfish, the male (which is much tinier than the female) is born with a highly developed sense of smell and no digestive system. His only mission in life is to find a female or die trying. Once he sniffs out a mate, he clamps onto her with his jaws, and there he stays for the rest of his life. Special enzymes break down the skin on her body and around his mouth so that they fuse together—and the male lives on getting nutrients from the female and providing sperm for her eggs.

I'm sticking with you, Babe!

8 What a Stink!

Take a deep breath. What do you smell? Maybe you can detect the faint odor of this morning's breakfast or of freshly mown grass. To animals, however, the world is filled with scents and odors that communicate important knowledge that they have no words to express. Sometimes, scent is used as a weapon to keep enemies at bay and sometimes, it's just a by-product of another bodily function. Whatever the case, these ten animals have perfected some of the most extreme smells on the planet.

#10 Dog

What do you do when you need to disguise your own scent in order to sneak up on prey? Roll around in something stinky! Wolves do it, and so do dogs—even pets that don't need to hunt for food. A dog's sense of smell is about a million times keener than a human's. When you see a dog sniffing around a tree trunk or fire hydrant, it's probably checking out the smell of urine left by another dog. One dog's waste can tell another dog about its sex, health, and even its mood.

#9 Turkey Vulture

Vultures have no sweat glands to help them cool off, so a few types, like turkey vultures, have figured out a stinky solution to their problem: They poop on their legs. There's a lot of moisture in bird droppings, and the moisture helps to cool off the bird. Ammonia in the droppings helps to kill bacteria, so it may be a disgusting habit (at least to humans), but it's not an unhealthy one.

Some dogs have been trained to recognize by smell when an epileptic is about to have a seizure minutes in advance, allowing the patient to take medication and get to safety. **THAT'S WILD!**

#8

Hooker's Sea Lion

Hooker's sea lions have bad breath. Really bad breath. These animals can eat about 60 pounds of fish a day. So what turns fresh fish into ferocious fish breath? Primarily the odorous gases released by digestive enzymes in their mouth and bacteria from fish rotting in their teeth. To top it all off, Hooker's sea lions get rid of indigestible fish parts by throwing the bits up, adding the heady aroma of vomit to the mix.

Hooker's sea lions are the deepest diving sea lions, descending as far as 1,500 feet.

THAT'S WILD!

Got a mint?

#7

Musk Ox

Musk ox are well known for their spectacularly stinky self-marketing program during mating time. The males pee on their feet to establish dominance and attract females! The boys will also roar, use intimidating postures, and butt heads to get the other males to back off. The stakes are big: Only the winner gets the right to breed with all the females.

#6

Hippopotamus

Who's the biggest party-pooper on the planet? Believe it or not, it's the hippopotamus. Male hippos are not only big, bad, and mean-tempered, but also have a novel way of showing who's boss. Hippos eat about 90 pounds of plants nightly. As a result, they make lots of green, goopy feces. And when rival males face off, they twirl their tails like propellers, showering each other with flying dung.

Male hippos cause more human deaths in Africa than lions and have even been known to bite a boat in half.

THAT'S WILD!

#5 Hyena

When you are a pack animal on the wide-open African savanna, how do you keep in touch with others in your pack and tell rivals to stay away? Hyenas have taken the wolf's ability to communicate through scent marking to its smelliest extreme. They use a stupendously stinky paste in their anal pouches to mark territory. This "hyena butter," as the locals call it, is so stinky that the smell stays put for about 30 days.

- Hyenas have such strong teeth and jaws that they can eat just about all animal parts, bones included.
- Contrary to popular belief, hyenas are very able hunters. In fact, lions frequently scavenge kills from hyenas.
- Baby hyenas are born with teeth.

THAT'S WILD!

SPECIAL REPORT: Hormonal Hyenas

The gender roles are reversed in hyena society, making the females dominant. In fact, males in the clan will not move toward food until the dominant females have fed. Scientists have noted that levels of hormones that promote aggressive behavior are higher in the alpha females than they are in the subordinate females. The result: The alpha females have more aggressive pups, behavior likely to increase their chances for success as adults. ●

#4 Wolverine

In North America, the weasel family developed its scent—a combination of anal secretions and urine—into a pungent spray. The wolverine, the largest of the weasel family, might not win a "stink-out" with its cousin, the skunk, but it still comes in pretty high on the stink scale. That's because it has a nasty habit of getting rivals to stay away from its caches of food by spraying it!

Giant Petrel

These large seabirds were actually called "stinkers" by whalers, who were totally grossed out by the birds' feeding habits. Giant petrels are the vultures of the Southern Ocean off Antarctica, feasting on the bodies of dead or dying penguins, bodies found at seal pupping sites, and the eggs and chicks of other seabirds. They also will eat fresh food like squid, fish, and shrimp. But if you get too close to nesting giant petrels, you'll get a whiff of the other reason these birds are so smelly. Many petrels will vomit on a predator, and because their diet is so smelly, their vomit is seriously awful. Worse, the vomit is so acidic that it can eat right through the special coating on feathers that make a bird waterproof—which can be deadly for the would-be predator.

- Giant petrels have been known to kill other large seabirds like albatrosses to get their eggs.
- Unlike most seabirds, giant petrels find most of their food on land rather than at sea.

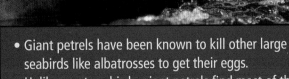

THAT'S WILD!

Don't you like my perfume?

#2

Skunk

Just one encounter with a skunk is enough to bring tears to your eyes. That's not just because it is one of the stinkiest animals on the planet. It's also because skunk spray can cause so much eye irritation that it can result in temporary blindness.

Stench warfare can be an extremely effective defense mechanism, especially for animals that don't run fast. However, most animals in the forest already recognize the skunk's distinctive black and white markings and will leave it alone. When it is threatened by a predator, however, a skunk's first instinct is to avoid confrontation. If that doesn't work, the skunk will hiss, turn its back, and raise its tail. And if that warning doesn't do the trick, it's stink-bombs away! And a skunk has high accuracy in hitting any target within a 7- to 10-foot range.

The reason a skunk doesn't immediately spray a predator is probably because it makes only enough of the spray for five or six uses, and it takes about ten days for its body to produce more.

- Skunks are said to be sociable, cuddly, and quite clean, and more and more people are adopting them as pets. Before breeders sell them, however, they do have the animals' scent glands removed.
- The skunks primary predator is the great horned owl—a bird of prey with a near nonexistent sense of smell.

THAT'S WILD

Millipedes, long, many-legged plant eaters, are relatively slow moving, so they've developed special chemical defenses against predators. Many millipede species exude an odor that is not only foul-smelling, but also packs a lethal punch—it's made of hydrogen cyanide, a gas that smells like bitter almonds and can kill. Cyanide gas prevents cells from taking in oxygen, causing them to die.

When threatened by a predator, a millipede mixes two chemicals together in reaction chambers along the sides of its body to make a liquid. Then it adds a special enzyme that converts the liquid into clouds of deadly gas that it lets out through tiny pores in its body. All it takes is seven one-millionths of a single ounce to kill a predator the size of a mouse. Making such a lethal substance, however, is so costly to the millipede in terms of energy that it will usually try to crawl away first. Some millipede species will even curl up into a ball, making them look too big to eat. But most predators have learned to leave millipedes alone—even birds, which generally don't notice smells.

- Even though the name millipede means "1,000 feet," most species only have between 80 and 400 legs. A rare millipede found in a tiny area of California has the most legs—about 750.
- Lemurs have figured out how to stimulate certain millipedes to produce a chemical that the lemurs then rub on themselves as an insect repellent!

THAT'S WILD!

9 Super Senses, Super Smarts

Animals with super powers? That's not so far from the truth. Lots of animals have developed an extremely specialized sense organ in order to locate food, spot enemies, or find mates from a distance. Other animals use their brains to solve similar challenges. And some creatures use both their brains and their senses. Get ready to meet ten of the most extreme problem-solving animals on the planet.

#10

Star-nosed Mole

Meet the star-nosed mole, named for the wacky-looking star of fleshy pink tentacles at the end of its nose. The star is what gives this mole its superior sense of touch. When a star-nosed mole is hunting for food, its tentacles move rapidly, touching things so fast they look like a blur. The star can touch 12 objects per second, and with tens of thousands of touch receptors crammed into those tentacles, a star-nosed mole can identify (and eat) a food item in mere milliseconds—as fast as the speed of thought.

#9

Moon Moth

When a female moon moth is ready to mate, she releases a tiny fraction of an ounce of chemicals called pheromones into the air. Smell receptors packed into the feathery antennae of a male can detect the faintest whiff of these pheromones from miles away, so he can track the female down—and fast! Why the rush? Adult moon moths live only to mate and reproduce, and die a week or two later. Since they have no mouth, adult moths can't even eat!

In one experiment, a caged female moon moth attracted 127 males from as far away as two miles in just three hours! **THAT'S WILD!**

Tarsier

This tiny mammal has the best sight in the forest, largely due to its huge eyes. In fact, it's the only animal with eyes that are literally bigger than its stomach! Tarsiers can see so well in the dark that they can leap a distance of more than 20 times their body length and stick a perfect (and accurate) landing. An extremely acute sense of hearing also helps to make this animal an excellent nighttime hunter.

Mantis Shrimp

Situated on the end of a stalk, each eye of a mantis shrimp can move independently of the other and has trinocular vision—so even if the animal loses one eye, it won't lose its trinocular vision. The mantis shrimp can also see ultraviolet and polarized light, which are invisible to humans. So much visual data gets processed by each eye that it bypasses the creature's brain and is fed directly into its nervous system. Scientists think this enhanced vision helps the shrimp see its prey, which is often transparent.

Shark

Super sight, super smell, super touch, super hearing—sharks have it all. What's most amazing is their highly developed electrosense, the ability to detect the electrical impulses of living creatures. Sharks have tiny jelly-filled pores in their skin that connect to electro-receptor cells. These cells enable them to "see" the electrical impulses of their prey, even when they lay hidden and unmoving in the sand. This sense sometimes causes sharks to attack objects like boats or shark cages. They confuse the electricity conducted by metal with that given off by prey.

Snow Monkey

If intelligence means taking information received through the senses and using it to learn new things, monkeys must rate highly on the intelligence scale. They are always learning new tricks. For example, take snow monkeys, who live in northern parts of Japan where it gets pretty cold. The monkeys watched people bathing in hot springs, and one day a monkey joined in. Pretty soon, all the monkeys learned to warm up in hot springs. Now it's considered part of snow monkey behavior.

Have I got some good gossip!

#4

Crow

It used to be thought that only humans were smart enough to use tools. Not so. Crows not only know how to use tools to retrieve food, but also have learned how to harness people and technology to help them. Many crows like walnuts but find the whole nuts difficult to crack. In Japan, some crows were seen to drop walnuts on a crosswalk and wait for cars to drive by and crush the nuts. The crows even learned to wait for the light to change and stop the flow of traffic before retrieving their treats.

No fair! You took the bigger piece!

How can you tell a crow from a raven? Ravens are visibly larger. A crow's tail feathers are cut straight across, while a raven's tail is shaped like a V. Their calls sound different, too. Check out this Web site to hear the difference: www.shades-of-night.com/aviary/difs.html

THAT'S WILD!

Pig

There's a lot of smarts packed into a domestic pig's stocky body. Although we raise them for their meat, these animals are quite complex. Smarter than dogs, according to some researchers, pigs can be trained to perform circus tricks, and they can solve puzzles and figure out how to open bolted doors on their own. They also have extremely good memories and are thought to have a basic language, consisting of grunts, sniffs, and other sounds, for communicating with other pigs.

Pigs not only have super smarts, but also superior senses. Their sense of smell is even more acute than a dog's. Because of this, female pigs, or sows, are used to ferret out a rare delicacy called truffles, a type of mushroom that grows underground near the foot of trees. Apparently, the truffles have the same smell as a boar (male pig) that is ready to mate. With 20,000 taste buds (three times the number humans have), pigs have a well developed sense of taste, too, so it's no wonder they're picky eaters and will often reject food if they don't like the way it tastes.

Pigs have been domesticated for thousands of years. Still, these animals quickly give up the traits that keep them dependent on humans when they go back to the wild—faster than any other animal. Perhaps that is the greatest mark of their intelligence. They are smart enough to survive wherever they find themselves.

Wall Street in New York City was named for the wall built in the 1650s to restrict the movements of lower Manhattan's loose pigs.

THAT'S WILD!

Come on in! The water's great!

Dolphin

Dolphins are actually whales with teeth, like orcas and sperm whales. Dolphins, however, are smaller, usually have a beak, and sport a brain as big as a human's. The presence of such a large brain with many folds suggests that dolphins are quite intelligent. Dolphins can perform amazing tricks; live in large, social groups; cooperate with other creatures and humans; recognize their own reflection in a mirror; and sometimes act deceitfully—which is considered extremely sophisticated behavior. Dolphins also communicate with each other using a wide range of clicks, whistles, and other sounds.

In addition to smarts, dolphins have extraordinary senses. First, there is the organ known as the melon. Dolphins (and all toothed whales, in fact) use the melon to send out sonic waves. Some can be powerful enough to stop prey cold—no harpoons (or hands) needed! Dolphins use echolocation to navigate, which is ideal for underwater situations, where sight can be unreliable.

- Dolphins are tool users, too! Some females in Australia have learned to wear sponges on their snout to protect themselves from sharp corals and stingers.
- Some dolphins have learned to cooperate with humans during runs of fish like mullet. They signal to let the fishers know when to cast their nets. In return, the humans give the dolphins part of their catch.
- Dolphins sleep by entering a state that allows one half of the brain to rest at a time.

THAT'S WILD!

#1 chimpanzee

There are two species of chimpanzee—common chimpanzees and bonobos. Both live in Africa, have a roughly human-sized brain, and share 95 to 99 percent of their DNA with humans. In fact, some scientists have proposed reassigning chimpanzees to the genus *Homo*, which would make them part of the same group as humans. After all, other species have been grouped together on the basis of less similarity than that between chimpanzees and humans. Chimpanzees make and use their own tools, have complex societies, and are able to communicate with one another through a wide range of vocalizations, including pants, hoots, grunts, and screams. They don't have language the way people do because their mouths and jaws are shaped differently. However, this difference hasn't prevented chimpanzees from learning human words and basic communication skills with the help of American Sign Language and computers that show signs. One animal, a bonobo named Kanzi, goes to Georgia State University and uses their computer. He not only understands the signs, but also can use them to respond in basic sentences. Other chimps have learned to talk through sign language and continue to remember the signs for people and objects over long periods of time.

Let's think about this for a minute.

- Captive chimpanzees can reach the age of 60, but Cheeta, the chimp star of the old movie *Tarzan*, turned 74 in 2006!
- Chimpanzees have opposable thumbs on both hands and feet.
- Chimpanzees are able to recognize the medicinal value of certain plants. The medicinal plants are only eaten by animals that appear sick or during times when infections are frequent.

THAT'S WILD!

10 All About Eating

Food, glorious food! Getting enough of it is an all-consuming activity for many animals. Depending on where the animals live and the hand nature has dealt them in the digestion department, many have found favorite foods that would be surprising to see on a human's dinner table. Dust? Clay? Poison? You name it and some animal is bound to eat it. Get ready to meet ten of the world's most extreme eaters!

#10

Hummingbird

These tiny birds process food so fast and expend so much energy in flight that they have to eat constantly or they'll die. They must typically eat up to two times their own weight in flower nectar every day. So it makes sense that while hummers visit hundreds of flowers daily, they rest up in between flights to conserve energy, and at night, while they sleep, they lower their rate of breathing and heart rate, which reduces their metabolism.

#9

Macaw

Leaves are a plant's food factories, and the fruits and seeds are its hope for the future, so some plants wage a fierce battle to keep animals from eating them. How do they do it? They load up their edible parts with toxins and unpleasant-tasting tannins. Enter the scarlet macaw. This species of parrot has developed a habit of eating clay from the sides of cliffs. The clay binds with the plant toxins so that the birds can excrete them safely, while retaining the useful nutrients.

Hummingbirds flap their wings 15 to 80 times per second, depending on the species.

THAT'S WILD!

Anyone seen Jerry?

#8

Tick

A tick lives off the blood of different host species. It doesn't have to eat often, but when it does, it totally pigs out. Some ticks can suck up 600 times their own weight in blood. What make ticks dangerous are the diseases they pass along to their hosts (humans included). Ticks are some of the biggest germ spreaders on the planet.

#7

Dust Mite

The largest ingredient in house dust is the dead cells of human skin. Dust mites live in people's nice warm houses (in rugs, upholstery, stuffed toys, and bedding), feasting on their old skin. Their food is even predigested for them by a common fungus! The mites that live in bedding get their moisture from the sleeper's sweat, saliva, and breath. No wonder some people have nightmares about aliens in the bedroom!

Experts say that 10 percent of the weight of a two-year-old pillow is dead dust mites and their droppings.

THAT'S WILD!

#6

Tiger Shark

Tiger sharks will eat just about anything—including non-food items, such as car license plates, cans, and plastic bottles. If the indigestible bits start to cause stomach trouble, the shark can solve the problem by spitting out its stomach contents—or even throw up its stomach then pull it back in! Along with great white sharks, tiger sharks have bad reputations as man-eaters. It may simply be a matter of chomp first, ask questions later, a type of feeding called "bite and spit." But while great whites generally do spit humans out, tiger sharks just keep chomping.

Dung Beetle

You may find this hard to believe, but there are critters out there that actually eat dung—by choice. There are thousands of species of dung beetles (also known as scarab beetles) all busily eating animal droppings. They either eat it themselves or roll it into a ball, lay an egg inside, and bury it, so the dung will serve as a food source for the baby beetle. Even after larger animals are finished with it, there's plenty of nutrition left in dung, and the plus for insects is that it's all predigested! A fresh dung patty can attract thousands of beetles at a time, and these busy beetles can whisk it all away in about two hours.

To ancient Egyptians, scarab beetles represented Ra, the sun god who rolled the sun across the sky and buried it each night.

THAT'S WILD!

Parrotfish form large groups of many females with one dominant male. When the male dies, the largest female changes color—and sex!

THAT'S WILD!

Polly want some algae?

#4

Parrotfish

Parrotfish are like the cows or sheep of the sea: herds of them graze the coral reefs of tropical waters. They don't eat grass, however, but algae, which they scrape off the stony skeletons of dead coral polyps. They use special teeth, fused together into a parrotlike beak (the origin of their name), for the algae scraping, but they still break off and swallow a lot of coral. What then? The fish have teeth in their throat that grind the stone into a fine powder that passes through the fish's system and comes out as sand. Just one fish can produce one ton of coral sand a year!

#3

Meerkat

The burrow-digging meerkat lives in one of the harshest habitats on Earth: the Kalahari Desert of Africa. Surviving in the Kalahari takes some special skills. Meerkats seem to be resistant to some types of venom and have learned ways to disable venomous prey, such as dragging a millipede along the ground to force it to secrete its poisonous gas before eating it, or biting off a scorpion's stinger before gobbling the animal up.

These skills aren't inborn, but taught to young meerkats by the adults in a colony. For example, an adult will give a scorpion that's already dead to a young meerkat. Next, it will remove a scorpion's stinger but give the living animal to the young. Finally, it will provide a living scorpion with stinger in place so that the young animals have to remove it themselves.

Meerkats have dark patches of fur surrounding their eyes that make their eyes look bigger, so they appear more threatening from a distance. The dark fur also helps to deflect the sun's glare. To learn more about meerkats, watch *Meerkat Manor* on Animal Planet.

THAT'S WILD!

A step to the left and a big kick to the right.

#2

Nudibranch

Colorful sea slugs, which are basically snails that have lost their shells, nudibranchs are some of the most fantastic-looking creatures in the ocean. Freed from their shells, which disappear when they take their adult form, they add on some amazing adornments, like ruffly mantles, feathery gills, and colorful tentacles.

Many of these are actually defensive adaptations. Sometimes, the colors serve as warnings to predators: "Stay away. We taste terrible," or "We're toxic!" Other times, the coloration helps the nudibranch blend into the bright colors of its habitat.

The cleverest of all the nudibranchs, however, are the ones that have harnessed the hunting system of a totally different creature for their own self-defense. Some tubular nudibranchs eat hydroids (animals like hydras, part of the same family as jellyfish) that have stinging cells used for stunning prey. The nudibranchs can somehow eat the stinging cells without firing them off or digesting them. Eventually, the cells become incorporated into the nudibranch's tentacles. So, quite literally, a hydroid's stingers are what's watching a nudibranch's back!

#1 Poison Dart Frog

If it wasn't for its highly specialized diet, this small, colorful frog would be an ordinary amphibian. But because it eats venomous ants and possibly beetles, the poison dart frog is transformed into one of the deadliest creatures on Earth. Without its powerful method of self-defense, this frog would easily end up on the dinner menu for the hordes of creatures that inhabit the Central and South American rain forests.

There are more than 200 species of poison dart frogs, and most of them are not terribly dangerous to animals or humans. Among the ones that are dangerous, though, is the golden poison dart frog. The poison in just one frog's skin is enough to kill 10 humans!

How did these frogs get their name? Native tribes in Central and South America have long been aware of the powerful substances in the frogs' skins. Some tribes, like the Chocó Indians of western Colombia, dipped darts into the frogs' skin secretions and shot the darts at prey with blowguns made from hollow tubes. One shot was enough to drop an animal, causing paralysis and death.

I dare you to kiss me.

- If you change the poison dart frog's diet to nontoxic insects, the frog will stop being poisonous.
- The skin and feathers of some pitohui, birds found in New Guinea, contain the same poison found in poison dart frogs.

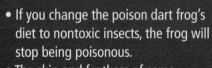
THAT'S WILD!

11 Horrors!

We want your pollen!

There are plenty of good reasons for humans to be afraid of lots of animals. Alone and without help from technology, humans might easily lose in confrontations with certain kinds of creatures. People have even spent a lot of time hunting down and exterminating many predatory animals. But is such destruction really necessary? Take a look at ten of the extreme creatures that horrify people the most and see what you think.

#10

Snake

Snakes cause nearly 40,000 human deaths every year. Not all snakes are deadly, but it can be hard to tell one kind from the other. Snakes use venom for both hunting and self-defense, so using it all up for self-defense could mean going hungry. Rattlesnakes, which are among the most venomous snakes in North America, use their rattle to scare away enemies. After all, if two shakes of a tail will scare someone off, there's no need to waste perfectly good venom.

#9

Bee

Bees are good because they pollinate flowers and make honey. But if a bee stings one of the two million Americans who are allergic to bee venom, he or she could go into shock and possibly die. Even people who aren't allergic can be harmed if they are stung by many bees. Honeybees send out chemical scents that alert the hive to a possible threat, sometimes leading to a mass attack. Africanized honeybees—a result of cross-breeding African bees with European bees—are extremely aggressive and likely to attack in great numbers, hence their reputation as "killer bees."

Sharks can have as many as 3,000 teeth—and they are constantly replacing old teeth with new, sharper ones.

THAT'S WILD!

My favorite restaurant!

#8 Shark

Just about everyone is afraid of sharks. The truth is that sharks are responsible for only about 100 or so human deaths a year—yet every year, humans kill 100 *million* sharks. Because of their fear, people hunt sharks relentlessly, even though they don't present all that much of a problem. Another stark truth: Unlike humans, sharks only kill to eat.

#7 Rat

Rats are the animals people love to hate. Humans are determined to exterminate rats, and rats are equally determined to survive. Naturally wary creatures, rats shy away from unfamiliar objects like traps. They've even built up a tolerance for what used to be lethal doses of rat poison. Only one tactic has ever shown real promise: shutting down their food supply. Rats live off garbage, and if people didn't make so much of it and secure it so poorly, there would be fewer rats.

May I please have another napkin?

#6 Komodo Dragon

Tales of fanciful monsters like dragons have been scaring people since the invention of the fairy tale. However, there is one dragon that's not a figment of the imagination. It's the Komodo dragon, the world's largest lizard, and its bite is deadly. It's not that the dragon has venom or is powerful enough to break its victim's neck. Rather, its serrated teeth are home to more than 50 different kinds of bacteria, some of which cause blood poisoning—even in large animals like water buffalo—and the bitten animal ends up sickening and dying.

Until they're about eight months old, baby Komodo dragons live in trees to avoid becoming lunch for older dragons!

THAT'S WILD!

Give me that veggie burger! Now!

#5

Spider

For the most part, spiders get a bum rap from humans. Without these helpful arachnids, we'd be waist-deep in insect pests, yet a lot of people are scared of spiders. In fact, psychologists think that just about everyone has a basic mistrust of these critters. But most of the 40,000 known species of spider have delicate jaws and short fangs—in other words, they just don't have the right equipment to inflict major injuries on people. And the venom they have is geared for insect prey, not humans.

#4

Gorilla

Gorillas are big and immensely powerful, and when they feel threatened, they will aggressively charge at intruders. So people might be forgiven for being scared of the gorilla. These peaceful primates are actually so shy that little was known about them until fairly recently. It took someone like Dian Fossey, a scientist who observed gorillas in the wild for several years, to bring back the truth about these gentle giants—that they are vegetarians that live together more peacefully than the smaller, more aggressive chimpanzees.

#3

Bat

Bats are another animal with a bad reputation that is largely undeserved. Experts say that one of the reasons people are so scared of bats is that they just don't know that much about them—after all, they are most active during the night, and many live in places like caves, which a lot of people think of as spooky. The bats that may swoop over your head aren't after you, they are after the bugs that you've stirred up while walking.

Vampire bats, however, are pretty creepy, so it's easy to understand why people are scared of them. These little animals are stealth hunters. They sneak up on animals like horses or cows that sleep in the open and make an incision with special teeth. An anticoagulant in their saliva keeps the blood flowing, which the bats then lap up. While vampire bats don't necessarily target people (apparently they dislike human blood, for the most part), they have been known to bite those who are sleeping out in the open.

- If a vampire bat can't get a blood meal every few days, it may approach another vampire bat in the colony and beg for some food. One bat will transfer the food to the other by mouth.
- Flying makes a vampire bat's getaway a little tricky. It has to pee out as much as it takes in or it can't lift off.

THAT'S WILD!

#2

Piranha

Piranhas are ferocious meat-eating fish that hunt in packs and can strip a large animal like a horse to the skeleton in just a few minutes, right? As is often the case, the truth about these famously fierce fish is more complicated.

When the river runs high and there's plenty of food, piranhas don't usually attack people. In fact, they are rather shy. Sure, they'll hunt for prey, but they are just as likely to scavenge off dead animals, and sometimes they'll even eat plants. Some species feed off the fins and scales of other fish (even other piranhas) instead of the meat. But when the river is low, piranhas get more aggressive and attack larger prey like capybaras (the world's largest rodents), pack animals, and people. Piranhas respond to noise and splashing rather than the smell of prey. And when they get going, they can attack with such ferocity that it looks as though the water is boiling.

- A *vegetarian* piranha? It's true. The pacu, a confirmed vegetarian, feeds on fruits and seeds that fall or get knocked into the river.
- Red-bellied piranhas have such sharp teeth that some Amazonian Indians use the teeth as knives. The fish loses and replaces its teeth throughout its life.

THAT'S WILD!

#1 Wolf

I don't see anyone else here!

No wonder wolves got a bad rep. Humans had good reason to be scared of them—wolves were everywhere, they're stronger than humans, and they run in packs. But it turns out that the wolves recognized people as competitors to be reckoned with, and healthy wolves knew enough to leave them alone.

People, on the other hand, were so spooked by the possibility of death by wolf that they very nearly hunted these animals to extinction. There are no wild wolves in the United Kingdom at all, although a reintroduction program is being considered. The wolf's range in Europe and Asia is only 25 percent of what it was. Only a few thousand wolves still live in North America. The good news is that populations in North America are recovering. Why the change? People now recognize some fundamental truths about wolves, such as:

- Most wolf attacks on record were by wolves with rabies, a virus that changes their normal behavior. As the spread of rabies decreased in Europe, so did the number of fatal wolf attacks.
- Healthy wolves have never caused a human death in the United States—as opposed to domesticated dogs, which have.
- When wolves attack people out of self-defense, human fatalities do not result.
- Wolves help keep populations of herd animals healthy by eating the unhealthy individuals.
- Wolves prefer wild animals to livestock, so they should not represent a problem for farmers.

12 Zombie Jamboree

Here are stories about ten extreme animals that suffer a "living death." For most of them, their "death" is anything but permanent. Sometimes, it's self-imposed to fool predators. Other times, it's a state of suspended animation that allows the animal to survive some extremely harsh environments, for extremely long periods of time. For others, however, the temporary "death" will turn into a permanent death.

My back's killing me!

#9

Opossum

The opossum, America's only pouched mammal (or marsupial), is a whiz at playing dead. When threatened, the opossum foams at the mouth and secretes a foul-smelling liquid from glands in its rear. It even loses consciousness. What's really amazing is that these responses are totally involuntary—the opossum can't control them. You can poke and prod an opossum in this state and nothing will happen. It's been known to remain comatose for as long as six hours before it recovers and walks away.

#10

Hog-nosed Snake

The first thing the western hog-nosed snake of North America does when confronted with a strange animal is rear back and take deep breaths to make itself look bigger. Then, with loud hisses, it attacks! But it's all a big bluff, because when the hog-nosed snake strikes, it doesn't even open its mouth. If attacking doesn't work, the snake goes belly up and fakes its own death. Special blood vessels in its mouth rupture, producing a foul stench that makes its "death" all the more believable. When the predator disappears, the snake rights itself and slithers away.

No, MY back's killing ME!

#8

Tarantula

You'd think a big spider like a tarantula could fight off all insect predators, but that's not the case. The female tarantula hawk wasp sniffs out a spider in its burrow and lures it out. After a sometimes fierce battle, the wasp paralyzes the tarantula with her stinger and drags it back into its own burrow or, if she's caught a male tarantula on the prowl, a burrow she digs herself. Then the wasp lays one egg on the spider and seals up the entrance. When the larva hatches, the still living spider provides it with plenty of fresh food.

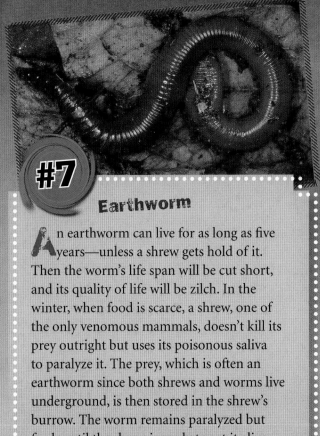

#7

Earthworm

An earthworm can live for as long as five years—unless a shrew gets hold of it. Then the worm's life span will be cut short, and its quality of life will be zilch. In the winter, when food is scarce, a shrew, one of the only venomous mammals, doesn't kill its prey outright but uses its poisonous saliva to paralyze it. The prey, which is often an earthworm since both shrews and worms live underground, is then stored in the shrew's burrow. The worm remains paralyzed but fresh until the shrew is ready to eat it alive.

#6

Ant

An ant with a lancet fluke inside is no longer master of its own body. The parasite forces the ant to march up on a blade of grass or a plant stem and stay there until it's eaten by a grazing mammal, such as a cow, rabbit, or deer. Inside the mammal, the fluke reaches its adult state and produces thousands of eggs, which are excreted in the mammal's dung. When a snail eats the dung, it gets some eggs, too. The eggs hatch inside the snail, and when the developing larvae irritate the snail, its body encases them in mucus. The snail coughs up the slime balls—which in turn are gobbled up by an ant because snail slime is its favorite food. And the cycle begins anew.

#5

Bear

Back in the Middle Ages, people thought that bears died when the weather turned cold because they disappeared. When the bears reappeared in the spring, it seemed like such a miracle that they became a symbol of regeneration and new life. Now we know that most bears hibernate during the winter, but that process is no less miraculous. Bears can stay in a state of suspended animation, where they don't need to eat or drink for up to six months. They even recycle their body wastes by converting them into usable proteins. What's even more miraculous: Female bears give birth to their cubs during hibernation.

Where's Goldilocks?

#4

Weta

They may look unsightly—sort of a cross between a giant cricket and a cockroach—but weta have the amazing ability to survive in just about any environment, no matter how extreme. Weta, flightless insects from the same family as crickets and grasshoppers, can be found in South America, Australia, and South Africa, but their biggest forms live in New Zealand.

On these islands, the insects grew large and heavy because they had no predators. So the weta spread out, some learning to live in trees, some in caves, and some in rocky crevices high in the mountains. Alpine weta have evolved to survive even the coldest weather. Because of certain proteins found in their blood that act like antifreeze, these weta can survive temperatures of 14°F (−10°C) without forming ice crystals, which would mean death for less hardy creatures.

Some weta can grow up to 8 inches long, legs included. That's some bug!

THAT'S WILD!

#3

Lungfish

Meet the lungfish—a creature that really can be a fish out of water. Supremely well adapted to its dual environment, the lungfish lives in areas that experience such extreme dry spells that the water virtually disappears. Living in a watery environment, fish have gills that help them extract oxygen from the water. But living in a place that is sometimes water-filled and sometimes dry is a problem for creatures that can only breathe in water. The lungfish, however, has special adaptations to deal with both situations.

Most fish have an organ called a swim bladder that helps them stay buoyant and upright in the water. In lungfish, this organ is modified to absorb oxygen directly from air and deal with waste removal during dry periods. Lungfish in Africa and South America survive dry spells by burrowing deep into the mud, curling up into a ball, and setting their metabolisms on super slow. The African species even secrete a special mucus coating that turns into a leatherlike protective cocoon. When all this happens, the lungfish's waste removal system switches on, turning their bodily wastes into reusable proteins. Some lungfish have been able to survive dry spells that last a few years.

Lungfish are part of the same group of animals that includes tetrapods, the ancient four-legged animals that first emerged from the oceans to become land-dwellers.

THAT'S WILD!

THAT'S WILD!

I've got a throat in my frog.

#2

Water-holding Frog

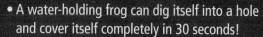

Beneath a dry lakebed in the Australian outback, there lives a frog that's been buried alive. It holds the secret of fresh water, even in the driest desert. The amazing water-holding frog spends most of the year underground. It buries itself in a muddy hole, sealed tight in a waterproof casing made up of its own shed skin, and slows its metabolism to prevent moisture loss. If necessary, it can stay there, safe in its little underground hidey-hole, for up to seven years! When heavy rains come at last and soak deep into the dry earth, the frog tears open its casing and eats it, emerges from its burrow, and lays its eggs in pools of still water left by the rains. The tadpoles quickly metamorphose into adults in order to be prepared to bury themselves during the next dry spell.

The Aboriginal people who have learned how to survive Australia's harsh dry periods know they can dig up these incredible frogs if they need a drink of fresh water. The frogs store the water in the bladder or in pockets under the skin. All that's needed is a gentle squeeze, and the animal releases its water, which is apparently very fresh. After the drink, the animal is released unharmed.

#1 Water Bear

Water bears, or tardigrades, are microscopic creatures that are found all over the world, even in polar regions. They move slowly on four pairs of clawed legs, and most of them suck the juices out of plants like mosses, while some eat bacteria. Some people think these tiny creatures look a bit like teddy bears. What makes these creatures so interesting to scientists are their incredible survival skills. Water bears need water to live and breed, but when the going gets tough and there is no water to be had, the water bear goes into hiding. Extreme hiding.

The water bear can stand to lose 99 percent of the water in its body. It retracts its legs and curls up into a little tiny barrel shape and, for all intents and purposes, it becomes indestructible. In its dry state, the water bear can withstand acid, solvents, altitudes of more than 3 miles, radiation, extreme heat (304°F/151°C), extreme cold (almost absolute zero), vacuums, and more. Yet all that's needed is a single drop of water to restore a water bear back to its normal self, without any of the tissue damage that most other species would experience. At an Italian museum, water bear specimens found in a sample of 120-year-old dried-up moss were tested to see if they could be revived. Researchers added water and—presto!—instant water bears!

SPECIAL REPORT:
Living on the Edge

The collective name for animals that survive in extreme places is "extremophiles." These creatures have made space scientists change their thinking. They once believed that atmospheres on other planets were too extreme to host life. Now they're not so sure. If extremophiles can withstand extreme cold, heat, and pressure, heavy metals, high concentrations of salt, acidity, and alkalinity here on Earth, there may indeed be extreme life forms on other planets. •

Glossary

alga an aquatic organism similar to a plant but lacking roots, stems, and leaves

amphibian a cold-blooded animal capable of living on both land and in water

anticoagulant a substance that prevents blood from clotting

antidote a remedy that counteracts the effects of a poison

arachnid an arthropod with four pairs of legs and a two-part body; spiders, mites, and scorpions are arachnids

arthropod an animal with a segmented body and jointed, external skeleton that must be shed in order to grow; insects, spiders, crustaceans, and centipedes are all arthropods

asexual related to reproduction that occurs without mating

bacteria simple one-celled microorganisms, some of which cause disease in humans and animals

bioluminescence visible light produced by a chemical reaction inside certain organisms; fireflies and many deep-sea animals produce bioluminescent light

blubber a thick layer of fat found in many marine mammals

brood animals that hatch at the same time and are cared for by the same mother

brood pouch an opening in certain animals' bodies where eggs or premature young stay to undergo further development

camouflage blending in with one's environment due to protective coloring

chemosynthesis a process that converts chemicals into energy

chitin a tough substance that makes up the shells of crabs, lobsters, and many insects

clone an offspring that is genetically identical to its parent

crop an enlarged pouch-like part of a bird's gullet in which predigested food is stored

dorsal fin the main, top fin located on the backs of fish and certain marine mammals

echolocation a sensory system that allows certain animals, such as bats and dolphins, to determine the direction and distance of objects based on echoes produced from their high-pitched cries

electrosense the ability to detect other organisms' electric impulses

extremophile an animal that has adapted to live under extreme conditions, such as hot springs

feces animal waste matter or excrement

fertilization the process by which a male sex cell (sperm) unites with a female sex cell (egg) to form the beginnings of an animal

glucose a sugar found in most plants and in animal tissue

habitat the environment in which an animal is normally found

honeydew a sweet liquid secreted by aphids and certain other insects

hormone a chemical substance produced in one part of an animal's body that travels to another part to work; hormones regulate various body functions, such as growth

host the animal or plant on which another animal lives

hydroid a class of sea animals that includes hydras, jellyfish, and Portuguese men-of-war

hydrothermal vent a hot spring or geyser from which heated fluids escape from cracks along the Earth's crust

implantation the process by which a fertilized egg is placed in the uterine lining of mammals

incubate to provide heat to eggs until they hatch

invertebrate an animal without a backbone

larva the early stage of metamorphosis in many insects when they appear as wingless, often wormlike, creatures

mammal a warm-blooded animal with a backbone; female mammals give birth to live young and produce milk to nourish them; humans, apes, and whales are all mammals

marsupial a mammal that is born prematurely and continues its development outside the womb; most marsupials are found in Australia and the Americas

molt to shed an exoskeleton or outer covering such as skin or feathers, which is replaced with new growth

neurotoxin a poison that acts specifically on nerve cells

parasite an animal that feeds and lives off another animal without contributing to the host animal's survival

pheromone a chemical secretion by a certain animals, especially insects, that is often used to attract mates

pollinate to transfer pollen in order to fertilize plants

predator an animal that hunts other animals for food

prey an animal hunted for food by other animals

scavenge to feed on garbage and/or dead animal remains

sperm the male sex cell

venom a poisonous substance made by certain animals and delivered through a bite or a sting

vertebrate an animal with a backbone

Resources to Find Out More

Books

Amazing Animals (Wild Animal Planet), by Michael Chinery, Lorenze Books, 2004

Lies (People Believe) About Animals, by Susan Sussman and Robert James, Albert Whitman, 1987

Encyclopedia of Animals, by Karen McGhee and George McKay, PH.D, National Geographic Society, 2006

Web Sites

Animal Planet
http://animalplanet.com
Official Web site for Discovery Channel's Amimal Planet, featuring fan sites for favorite series, videos, pet guides, games, interactives and much more.

Extreme Science
http://www.extremescience.com
Features all that is extreme in the natural world, including animals, and includes links of where to go for more information.

Animal Diversity Web
http://animaldiversity.ummz.umich.edu
Searchable Web site for finding information on all kinds of animals.

Photo Credits

Index